D0870586

New Currents in Western Buddhism

For thirty years Sangharakshita has been playing an important part in the spread of Buddhism throughout the modern world. He is head of the Western Buddhist Order (Trailokya Bauddha Mahasangha), and is actively engaged in what is now an international Buddhist movement with centres in thirteen countries worldwide. When not visiting centres he is based at a community in Norfolk. His writings are available in eleven languages.

New Currents in Western Buddhism

The Inner Meaning of the Friends of the Western Buddhist Order

Sangharakshita

Windhorse Publications

Published by Windhorse Publications
136 Renfield Street
Glasgow G2 3AU

From a series of talks delivered in 1979
in Auckland, New Zealand

Cover design Dhammarati

The picture on the cover shows Amitayus,
the Buddha of Infinite Life, traditionally
associated with the Western direction

Printed by F. Crowe & Sons, Norwich

British Library Cataloguing in Publication data
Sangharakshita, *Bhikshu, Sthavira, 1925—*
New Currents in Western Buddhism
1. Western world. Buddhism
I. Title
294.3091821

ISBN 0-904766-46-2

Contents

Editor's Preface

In 1967 Sangharakshita, newly returned from a twenty year sojourn in India, launched an entirely new Buddhist movement in the West. Since its first stirrings, in a tiny basement in central London, the Friends of the Western Buddhist Order has developed into a worldwide spiritual community, encompassing the lives of thousands. While the activities, institutions, and all the day to day richness of that movement are just hinted at in the following pages, we are presented instead with a kind of informal manifesto, a first hand account of Sangharakshita's reasons for establishing not only a new Buddhist movement, but a new—he would say radical—*kind* of Buddhist movement.

Buddhism is still something of a stranger to the West. It is little more than a hundred years since Sir Edwin Arnold's *The Light of Asia* brought it to the attention of a reasonably wide English-speaking public. For decades thereafter it remained little more than an object of detached scholarly interest and investigation.

Although the 1920s and '30s saw the emergence of a few societies and organizations whose work inspired sympathy and sometimes a little practice, it has only been in the last twenty or thirty years that Buddhism has emerged as a serious option for Westerners seeking a path of spiritual growth.

Even so, it is already possible to declare that Buddhism is here to stay. Enough people are now interested in it, enough people are seriously practising its teachings, and enough people are dedicating their lives to the creation and direction of Buddhist institutions to suggest that we are at the beginning of an era when the influence of Buddhism will make a significant contribution to life in the modern world. Clearly, Buddhism has come to the West not as just one more outlandish 'cult' doomed to enjoy its brief flash of popularity before returning to obscurity, but, deservedly, as a substantial and significant force. Buddhism is after all an older spiritual tradition than Christianity and Islam. For millennia it spread throughout the Far East focusing and nurturing the spiritual aspirations of hundreds of millions of people. That it should have gained a foothold in the West—and thus in the wider Westernized world—is a matter of considerable historic consequence.

As a universal teaching, Buddhism addresses itself to human beings in all places and at all times. It does not do this by offering a set of inflexible, 'divinely inspired', dogmas and rules to be revered and obeyed even at the expense of reason, doubt, or cultural context. Rather, through the medium of wise, sensitive, and creative individuals, it looks at the local variants of the human condition, and makes suggestions— about what is wrong, what is missing, and about how things could be better.

So far as recorded history is concerned, Buddhism took its first look at our world through the eyes of one man, Gautama the Buddha. That was two-and-a-half-thousand years ago in ancient India. Looking about him, the Buddha saw much pointless suffering; he saw greed, hatred, and delusion; he saw ignorance leading to wasted potential, wasted life. But he also saw that things didn't have to be like that. He knew that human beings had the capacity for wisdom, compassion, and freedom, and that, with effort and with guidance, they could liberate themselves from their woes just as he had done. These were the broad generalities, and they apply as much today as they did then.

But there were also the details. Meeting, talking with, and befriending his contemporaries, the Buddha saw exactly *how* and in what precise forms the evils of greed, hatred, and delusion so ensnared the people around him, and indicated how those people could live and conduct themselves—from moment to moment—in such a way as to free themselves and realize their magnificent potential. Again, many of these more specific teachings remain valid today and are still worth following, even to the letter. But much has also changed. The world is a different place, and while we 'moderns' may share many essential—indeed the most important—human traits with our ancient Indian predecessors, we live in a very different society; our psychological, social, cultural, and spiritual context and conditioning are quite different. What would the Buddha see today? And what would he have to say to us? Surely there would be new emphases, new warnings, fresh responses, and at least a few more appropriate and specific prescriptions?

So far as Buddhism is concerned there is nothing new in this. The world has been changing ever since the Buddha passed away. The India in which Buddhism went on to flourish became a different place to that in which Siddhartha Gautama had taught. Then, as the centuries passed, China, Sri Lanka, Tibet, Thailand, Vietnam, Indonesia, Japan—many, many lands— each confronted Buddhism with the challenge of adapting itself to dramatically new contexts. And yet, adapt it did. Though its call and its fundamental message remained the same, the language, the symbols, and many matters of detail through which it expressed itself, were different. Hence, for example, a Japanese

Buddha image takes the form of a Japanese man; a Thai image of a Thai, and so on. Time and time again, Buddhism so thoroughly succeeded in integrating itself with its host cultures that one could be forgiven for failing to guess from appearances where—on earth—its original source might lie.

If we look at the history of Buddhism we will see that that process of integration to a new time or a new place has almost always been made possible—if not entirely effected—by the genius of just a few talented and inspired individuals. One thinks, for instance of Nagarjuna, of Padmasambhava, of Bodhidharma, of Chih-i. Such people were the channels through which the current of Buddhism communicated itself to a new generation. Although well versed in the formal teachings and traditions of Buddhism, these men were often revolutionaries, writing astonishing, almost revelatory, texts, founding new schools of philosophy and practice, transforming never the essence but rather the outward mode of that current so that it might make a more effective connection with its new audience.

Of course it is far too early to claim that Buddhism has made a home for itself in the West; the process of integration has barely begun. And if history is anything to go by, it could be a couple of hundred years before we will get any clear idea of the form, or forms, that

Buddhism will finally take in the West. The great geniuses who will write the texts, create the art-forms, and build the communities that will allow people to approach Buddhism as if it had always been a Western phenomenon have probably not yet been born. Even much of the raw material for their meditation, contemplation, and visionary experience lies waiting for attention, or even discovery.

Nevertheless, the fact that Buddhism has emerged from the soup of oriental exoticism that characterized the sixties and early seventies, the fact that new translations of, and commentaries upon, ancient Buddhist texts are appearing at an accelerating rate, and the fact that the numbers of its followers are steadily increasing, suggests that the process has begun, and is unlikely to be reversed. And such facts must also suggest that we already have among us at least a few notable 'transformers', a few individuals who are able to look upon our Western world with truly Buddhist eyes, and speak with the authentic voice of the Dharma.

Sangharakshita is such a man. His creation, the FWBO, is itself still young and cannot presume to offer itself as any kind of final answer to the challenge of bringing Buddhism 'home' to the West. But it is hard to think of an answer that will be able to ignore the points that he makes in the talks that are recorded here.

By identifying the great spiritual predicament of our times as the threatened extinction of the individual, by warning us of the need to distinguish between essential Buddhism and its various cultural manifestations, and by urging us to build our Buddhist institutions upon the foundations of wholehearted commitment and spiritual friendship, he has set an agenda that will be ignored only at the risk of Buddhism's survival. That he has established a spiritual movement which attempts to put this agenda into practice makes the FWBO of interest to all who care about the fate of Buddhism in the West.

For those who feel anxious about the survival of the individual—especially of their own individuality—and who wish to nurture and unfold their potential as individuals, then I can only imagine that Sangharakshita's manifesto will excite far more than interest. If you are such a person, then you will no doubt take heart in the knowledge that Sangharakshita's views have taken form in a community of people who are actively trying to engage with them in their daily lives. That community is open to all. If you want, you can join it. After all, the adventure has only just begun.

Nagabodhi
Vimalakula Community
March 1990

The Individual and the World Today

These three talks are about the Friends of the Western Buddhist Order (FWBO), a new spiritual movement affiliated to the great tradition which we know as Buddhism. In referring to the FWBO as a spiritual movement, I am using the word 'movement' advisedly, deliberately avoiding such terms as 'organization', 'society', or 'association', and particularly the word 'group'. I am avoiding these terms because I will not be talking about just another organization, society, or group, but about something I can only describe as a 'current' of positive, emotional, and spiritual energy. In this context the word 'current' seems particularly appropriate. The word is often associated with electricity; if you touch an electric current, you get a shock. If you touch Buddhism you will also get a shock, and if you touch the FWBO, you will certainly get a shock. So the FWBO is a current of spiritual energy which moves from higher to ever higher levels of being and consciousness. It is a current which, with our co-operation, can take hold of us and give us that shock, even radically transform our lives—not only individually, but collectively.

The FWBO is a new spiritual movement first of all in the sense of being comparatively recent; it was founded only in 1967. It is also new in the sense that it is different from existing Buddhist groups in the West; in what way it is different we shall see later on. But the inner meaning of this new movement is revealed in its name, the Friends of the Western Buddhist Order, and in these three talks I am going to explore the meaning of that name. I will try to explain in what sense the FWBO is a movement of *Friends*, in what sense it is a *Western* movement, in what sense it is *Buddhist*, and in what sense it is an *Order*. For the sake of convenience, however, I will not be dealing with them in that order. I will be dealing first of all with the word 'Western', then with the word 'Buddhist', and finally with the words 'Friends' and 'Order' together.

In what sense is our new Buddhist movement *Western?* The FWBO was founded in the UK, just a few hundred yards from Trafalgar Square, in the very heart of London. It started in a tiny basement not more than twelve feet by fourteen, underneath a shop in Monmouth Street. Seven or eight of us used to meet there just once a week, on a Thursday evening. We would meditate for an hour, and then go home. That was how the

FWBO began. That was the little seed from which everything sprang. At the moment* we have about twenty public centres, some twenty residential communities, about thirty Right Livelihood business organizations, and we have spread to a number of countries. But we started—almost like mushrooms—in that rather small dark basement in central London.

The FWBO was started in the West, in the midst of a particular kind of society, even of a particular kind of civilization. This was certainly not the sort of civilization I had been living in in India for twenty years. It was in fact a civilization which differs from all previous civilizations in history. Above all, it differs in being both secularized, and industrialized. Of course, although this 'Western' civilization originated in the West, it is certainly not confined to it. In the course of the past 150 years or so it has spread to most parts of the globe. Although there are signs that this process is being resisted, sporadically, in one or two of the Islamic states, the world of today is a Western world, a world which is either Westernized or in process of Westernization, which is to say of secularization and industrialization. So when I say that the FWBO is Western, I do not mean that it just happens to be geographically located in the

---

*This talk was delivered in 1979

West, or that it was started, geographically speaking, in the West; I mean that it has arisen under the conditions of secularized and industrialized Western civilization. And it is with those conditions that the FWBO tries to cope. It tries to make the Buddhist way of life, the spiritual life, even—to drop all such terminology—the truly human life, possible, under these conditions.

The FWBO is therefore Western in the sense that it is concerned with the world of today, not with the world of yesterday, however bright that world may have been in some respects. Nor is it primarily concerned with the world of traditional religious culture. That world is a very beautiful world; I recently saw something of it in India and among my Chinese Buddhist friends in Malaysia. But that world has gone, it seems, for ever. The FWBO does not hark back to this beautiful, romantic, traditional, religious culture of the past; it looks forward. In this sense too it is young and new.

The world today has certain special problems, problems that did not exist in the past quite in the way that they exist now. These problems are not entirely new, but they happen to be more acute now, and confront us in a more urgent form—which means that their solution has become more urgent. You may immediately think of economic problems, or ecological problems, according to your particular interest, but the biggest problem of all, at least in human or spiritual terms, is the problem of the *individual*: the survival of the individual.

It is very difficult for the individual to survive nowadays. It is very difficult for the individual to grow and develop. And that which threatens the survival of the individual is clearly, in one word, the *group*. We could therefore say that the FWBO is Western in the sense that it is a spiritual movement of Buddhist origin which is concerned with the protection of the individual from the group.

That the individual—as such—needs to be protected might be a new idea to some people. We are familiar with the idea that children should be protected; we are even familiar with the idea that animals should be protected. But what about the individual? We sometimes forget that, nowadays, the individual too needs to be protected. The individual is threatened by the group, is threatened, even, with extinction.

By now you will have realized that I am using the terms 'group' and 'individual' in a rather special way. To explain what I mean I will have to go back a little in history, even into prehistory, and attempt a few definitions.

The group, of course, came before the individual, before the 'true individual'. Anthropologists tell us that Man has always lived in groups; the group was necessary to survival. This was true not only of Man but of all his pre-hominid ancestors as well: they all lived in groups of various sizes, containing anything from a dozen to two or three dozen members of various ages, and of course of both sexes. In this way they formed a sort of extended family group. This pattern was followed by Man, but with the difference that in the case of Man, the group gradually became bigger. Extended families merged to form tribes, tribes merged to form nations, nations founded states, and states even merged to form empires. This process extended over a period of many hundreds of thousands of years, gradually accelerating towards the end when we reach the period of recordable, datable history, which begins around 8000 BCE.*

Whether the group was large or small, in principle it remained unchanged. We can therefore define the group as a collectivity organized for its own survival, in which the interests of the individual are subordinated to those of the collectivity. The group, or collectivity, is also a power-structure in which the ultimate sanction is force. The group did not just make survival possible for its members; in the case of humans,

---

*Buddhists and other non-Christians do not use the abbreviations AD—'Year of our Lord'—and BC. They refer to years under the accepted dating convention as either CE (Common Era) or BCE (before Common Era).

it made it possible for them to enjoy higher and higher levels of material prosperity and culture. It made possible the emergence of folk art and ethnic religion; it made possible the emergence of civilization. But there was a price to be paid by the proto-individual, and that price was conformity with the group. The individual was regarded as being essentially a *member of the group*. The individual had no existence separate from the group, or apart from the group.

Let me give you an illustration of this from my own experience. Living in India for twenty years, I made many Hindu friends. Some of them, being very orthodox and rather old fashioned, used to be rather puzzled by the fact that I did not have a caste. Sometimes they would ask me, 'What is your caste?' because, in their view, I *had* to belong to a caste. When I told them that I did not have a caste, first of all because I was born in England, where we don't have caste, and secondly because I was a Buddhist, and in Buddhism we do not recognize the system of hereditary caste, they would say, 'But you *must* have a caste! Every human being must have a caste.' They could not conceive of someone who did not belong to one of the two thousand or so castes of Hinduism. They could not conceive of someone who did not belong to a group of some kind. There is something a little parallel to this in the West in that we cannot conceive of someone who is not of a particular nationality. But caste is even harder, even stricter, than that.

For the person who is essentially a member of the group, an individual—who does *not* belong to the group, whose being is not totally submerged in the group—is rather difficult to conceive. Because such a person is essentially a member of the group, he does not think for himself, he thinks and even feels just as the group does, and acts as other members of the group act. It does not even *occur* to him that he can do anything else. It does not *occur* to an orthodox Hindu that you need not have a caste. Whether we are talking about pre-historic times or nowadays, a group member, as such, is perfectly content with this state of affairs, because the group member is not an individual—not in the sense of being a *true* individual. He or she may have a separate body, but there is no really independent mind, no independent consciousness. The group member shares in the group consciousness, so to speak. We can call this sort of individual a 'statistical individual'. He can be counted, he can be enumerated, but he doesn't really exist as an individual in the true sense. He is simply a group member.

However, at some stage in Man's history, something remarkable happened. A new type of consciousness started to develop, a type of consciousness that we usually call 'reflexive consciousness', or self-consciousness, or self-awareness. Reflexive consciousness can be contrasted with 'simple consciousness'. With simple consciousness, you are aware of sights, you are aware of sounds, you are aware of trees, houses, people, books, flowers, and so on, but you are not aware of *being aware*. But in the case of reflexive consciousness, consciousness as it were doubles back upon itself, and one is *aware of being aware*.

When one is aware of being aware, one is conscious of oneself as an individual, conscious of oneself as separate from the group. One is conscious of one's ability to think and feel and act differently from the group, even against the group. An individual of this type is a true individual. Such a person is not only self-aware but is emotionally positive, full of good will towards all living beings. He is also spontaneous and creative because he is not determined in his thinking, feeling, or acting, by previously existing mental, emotional, and psychological patterns—whether his own or those of other people. The true individual is also responsible, aware of his own needs, aware of others' needs, and prepared and willing to act accordingly.

True individuals started appearing on the stage of history in relatively large numbers in the course of what we call—to use Karl Jaspers's term—the Axial Age. This Axial Age, a sort of crucial turning point in human history, was a three hundred year period extending very roughly from around 800 BCE to around 500 BCE. The true individuals who started to emerge during this period appeared in Palestine, Greece, Persia, India, and China, in fact in most of the great centres of civilization. Some of them were great thinkers, others were prophets and mystics; others again were poets, sculptors, and founders of religions. In Palestine we have such figures as the prophets Isaiah, Jeremiah, and Amos, as well as the unknown author of 'The Book of Job'. In Greece, we have Pythagoras and the great philosopher Plato; we have the Attic dramatists, the great poet Pindar, the sculptor Phidias, and so on. In Persia we have the prophet Zoroaster. In India we have the Upanishadic sages like Yagnavalkya; we have Mahavira, the founder of Jainism, and we have the Buddha. In China we have Confucius and Lao Tse, the two most important individuals to arise in the whole history of Chinese culture. Of course, some of these individuals went far beyond the stage of mere self consciousness. At least some of them developed what I have called 'Transcendental consciousness', and even 'Absolute consciousness'.

In this way, the Axial Age was a period of efflorescence of the true individual. Indeed, from this time onwards we can see two factors at work in human cultural, religious, and spiritual history. On the one hand there is the individual, and on the other hand there is the group.

Between the true individual and the group there was always a certain creative tension, the group pulling one way—in the direction of conformity—and the individual pulling the other—in the direction of nonconformity, of freedom, of originality, of spontaneity. In this dialectical relationship, the group provided the individual with his raw material. We find this, for example, in Greek drama. Here, certain myths and legends, themselves a product of the collective unconscious, provided the dramatists with stories which they adapted in such a way as to give expression to their own highly individual vision of existence. In this way the individual influenced the group, reacted upon the group, raising the statistical individuals who still belonged to the group, at least momentarily, to a higher level, bringing them closer to true individuality.

This relationship was in force for about two thousand years. On the whole it was a lively and a healthy one. Sometimes it broke down, as when the medieval Catholic Church started persecuting those 'heretics' who dared to think differently from the Church. (By this time, of course, the Church was no longer a spiritual community, as it had once been to some extent, but simply a religious group, a sort of ecclesiastical power structure.) But on the whole, the relationship between the true individual and the group continued fairly healthy for about two thousand years. Generally speaking, the group at least tolerated the individual—provided he did not impinge too uncomfortably upon the group. During the last two hundred years, however, a change has taken place to such an extent that a serious imbalance now prevails between the individual and the group. There are various reasons for this, but I will only summarize some of the more important ones.

To begin with, the population of practically every country in the world has greatly increased in recent years. During the twenty years I spent in India, for instance, the population of that country doubled! Because we have so many more people in the world, almost everywhere, it has become much more difficult to get away from one's fellows, much more difficult to get away from the group. This is especially the case in small, densely populated countries like Holland and the United Kingdom, and in some parts of the bigger countries.

Secondly, there is the increase in the power of the corporate state. Today's corporate state, we may say, is the group *par excellence*, and it controls so many aspects of our lives. In most countries, this control is increasing rather than decreasing. These corporate states now divide the whole world between them. There is no portion of the Earth's land surface which is not controlled by one or another corporate state, and they have even started staking out claims to the sea. There used to be some nice empty spaces, of 'terra incognita', between them, where you could go if you wanted to get away from the state. But those spaces no longer exist; there are no spaces anywhere in the world where no state exercises any authority. Every individual has to belong to a state, whether they like it or not. From time to time we hear about a few miserable people who have been declared stateless. Their condition is considered a terrible calamity because, these days, you just have to belong to a state. You have to have a passport, for without one you cannot travel from one state to another. This is a fairly recent development; passports came into general use only after the First World War. Before that it was not so necessary to have one. Now they are really indispensable.

Thirdly there is the growth of modern technology. This is in many ways a helpful development, but it has its disadvantages. It means that, among other things, the corporate state can now keep track of its citizens far more efficiently. A computer system can be set up to tell its operators a person's date of birth, when he or she last paid taxes, how many parking offences they have ever committed, where they spent their holiday last year, whether they have ever had measles, and so on. With this information at its fingertips, the state finds it much easier to exercise control over the individual.

Fourthly, there is our higher standard of living. This too is a blessing up to a point, but it does make us dependent on the group. We are dependent on the group for such good things of life as motor cars and television sets, not to speak of petroleum and electricity, since it is very doubtful whether we could produce these things by ourselves. Generally, we are so helpless, so dependent, that we cannot even grow our own food, or make our own clothes. The general principle would therefore seem to run thus: the higher our standard of living, the bigger and more complex the state to which we have to belong—and, therefore, the more control it exercises over our lives and the less freedom we have. There is something a little paradoxical about this. If we have a car, for instance, we have greater freedom in the form of more personal mobility. But that freedom is taken away from us in certain other respects by the fact that, in order to possess and to drive a car, we have to be part of a society which is geared to the production of cars—which may not necessarily be the best kind of society.

For these reasons we can now see that there is an imbalance between the individual and the group.

Now I have said that the corporate state is the group *par excellence*. But within the corporate state there are many other smaller groups. The corporate state is in fact a sort of interlocking system of groups, some of which are very powerful indeed when set against the individual. There is the political party, the trades union, the chamber of commerce, the church, the bank, the school. Some of these impinge on us in certain respects more strongly and more directly than does the corporate state itself. The result is that we are left with a virtually powerless individual in a virtually all-powerful state. The group has practically overwhelmed the individual, who feels, very often, that he is quite unable to influence the group, even in those matters which most closely concern his own life.

This is the state of affairs in the world today, especially in the Western democracies, in the old Communist states, and in various military dictatorships. It is a state of affairs which is becoming more and more widespread. And the result is that the true individual is dissatisfied. The 'statistical individual', very often, is not dissatisfied; very often he is happy with what the group provides, whether it is bread and circuses, as in the case of ancient Rome, or motor cars and television sets as is the case today. His only complaint is that he would like to have more of them more frequently! But the true individual is frustrated. In extreme cases, his frustration may sometimes find expression in violence. We know that violence is on the increase in our cities—and I am certainly not saying that frustration of the kind I've mentioned is the sole cause of this violence—but it is certainly one factor. What, then, are we to do?

To begin with, and above all, we have to restore the balance between the individual and the group. This means that we need a philosophy, a way of looking at things, that can provide the perspective within which we will be able to see the possibility of restoring the balance. We need a philosophy that recognizes the value of the individual, a philosophy that shows the individual how to grow, how to be a true individual. This is where what nowadays we call Buddhism (but which calls itself, in its own habitat, the *Dharma*) comes in.

Buddhism places the individual in the very forefront of its teaching. The Buddha's teaching is concerned solely with the individual, both alone and in free association with other individuals. It shows the individual how to grow, shows him or her, by means of actual methods, how to develop awareness, how to develop emotional positivity, how to live spontaneously and creatively, how to accept responsibility for oneself and for others, how, in other words, to be more and more of a true individual.

Gautama the Buddha, the original teacher, was and is an example of a true individual. He was an individual of the highest kind: an *Enlightened* individual. He was an individual who had developed not only reflexive consciousness, but also 'Transcendental' consciousness and 'Absolute' consciousness.

If we take even a cursory glance at the Buddha's life we can see how the Buddha's individuality demonstrated itself right from the start. Quite early in his life he cut himself off from the group; that was the first step he took of any significance. He left his parents, left his wife and child, left his city, left his tribe, and gave up his social position to wander alone from place to place. Occasionally he joined various religious groups and cults, but in the end he cut himself off from them too. They too were hindrances, they too were groups. He was left entirely alone—in a way that perhaps no one had ever been alone before. Being alone, he was able to be himself; being himself, he was able to be an individual; being an individual—looking at things as an individual, seeing things as an individual—he was able to see the Truth for himself, able to experience it for himself. Being able to see the Truth, he was able to become what we call a Buddha, an Enlightened individual. And having become an Enlightened individual, he was able to help others to become such. From that moment, we may say, the power of the group, the power of 'Mara'—the power of the gravitational pull of conditioned existence—was diminished.

In the Buddha's day the power of the group was perhaps not so great as it is today, but the Buddha's teaching and example were needed all the same. It is needed, we may say, whenever and wherever the survival of the individual is threatened, wherever there is an imbalance between the individual and the group, especially when that imbalance is as extreme as it is in the world today. There is no political or economic solution to such a problem. There is only a *spiritual* solution, a solution which takes the individual into account. If put into operation, that solution will of course have political and economic implications and consequences, but it has to be a solution that respects and emphasizes the value of the individual.

This is a radical view of things. After all, how many people respect the individual? You can meet so many people who do not respect you as an individual, who don't even *see* you as an individual. You can go into a shop or into a government office and try to deal with the people there. They do not see you as an individual; they see you as a sort of public zombie who has just drifted in. But the solution we need is a solution that *sees* the individual, that respects the individual, that allows the individual, even, to make his own mistakes, that does not hold the individual's hand all the time. This attitude is very well illustrated by an incident in the Buddha's life.

A brahmin once came to see the Buddha and asked whether he taught all his disciples the way to Nirvana *equally*. When the Buddha affirmed that he did, the Brahmin asked, 'But do they all, equally, *attain* Enlightenment?'

When the Buddha replied that some did, while others did not, the Brahmin was again rather puzzled and asked, 'Well, why is this? If they all get the same teaching, why don't they all realize Nirvana?'

The Buddha therefore gave him the following example: 'Over there,' he said, 'is the city of Rajagriha. Now, you know the city of Rajagriha; you know the way to the city of Rajagriha. So suppose two men come to you and both ask, "Please tell me the way to Rajagriha". And suppose you give quite detailed instructions: "Go along this road, pass that bush, turn that corner, go through that grove of mango trees, and then you'll get to the city." Suppose you give both of them these directions, and suppose one follows your directions and arrives, but the other does not follow your directions and does not arrive, because he makes a mistake, would it be your fault? Would you be to blame for that?'

'No,' said the Brahmin. 'If, after I had given the proper directions, one of them found the way but the other did not, it wouldn't be any fault of mine. I wouldn't be to blame. I am only the shower of the way. I only give directions.'

'It is the same in my case', said the Buddha, 'I am only a shower of the way.'

The Buddha is only the shower of the way, but it is up to the individual to follow that way, to decide for himself whether he is going to follow that way or not. We may say that this attitude shows tremendous respect for the individual. It shows great confidence in the potential of the individual. It shows an appreciation of the fact that the individual cannot be forced. He must *want* to change; he must *want* to develop. All that one can do is show him *how*, show him an example, encourage him, and, if one can, inspire him. But one can do no more than that. You can't force him, you can't bribe or threaten him; you can only show him the way. That is to say, if you are an individual, and are trying to deal with him as an individual, then you can only show him the way and leave it to him to follow or not to follow.

This attitude is the basis for Buddhism's well known spirit of tolerance. Buddhism is deeply conscious of human differences, deeply conscious of the fact that we are not all the same. We each have our own temperaments, characters, and our different ways of looking at things. We therefore have to be allowed to develop, each one of us, in our own manner. This is why, in the whole of its 2,500-year history, Buddhism has never persecuted anybody for their beliefs. There is no such thing as heresy in Buddhism.

There are such things as 'wrong views', views which hold us back and prevent us from developing, but these wrong views are to be corrected—if they are to be corrected at all—by discussion and not by force. Force has absolutely no place in Buddhism, no place in the spiritual life.

At this point, somebody might raise an objection. While agreeing that there is a serious imbalance between the individual and the group which needs to be corrected by spiritual means, they may nevertheless ask why we have to bring in Buddhism. Why should we not do it with the help of Christianity, which is after all traditionally the religion of the West?

I personally think that there are three main reasons why Christianity cannot help us correct the imbalance between the individual and the group. The first of these is that Christianity is on the side of the group. That Christianity has no respect for the individual is amply demonstrated by its history. Whenever and wherever Christianity has gained political power it has persecuted those who think differently, those who try to be individuals. We have only to think of the enormities perpetrated by the Inquisition, of the horrors of the Albigensian crusade, of the wars of religion in Europe in the sixteenth and seventeenth centuries, of the burning of witches—that is to say old women—at the stake. (Why were they burnt? Because the Bible says, 'Thou shalt not suffer a witch to live.') Even today, in democratic countries, Christian pressure groups are trying to get laws passed which would compel non-Christians to conform to Christian ideas of right and wrong.

Secondly, Christianity believes in God. It believes in a supreme being, an all-powerful, all-knowing creator of the heavens and the Earth. Buddhism does not believe in God. It teaches that belief in the existence of God is a view that prevents us from developing as true individuals. What is God, after all? If we forget the theological or the more abstract philosophical definitions, and just try to look at God more realistically, more psychologically and existentially, then we must conclude that God is simply the most powerful member of the biggest conceivable group. And we find, in fact, that God enforces group values—or is represented as enforcing group values—such as obedience, conformity, and respect for the powers that be.

Thirdly, people are encouraged to fear God. They are encouraged to feel guilty if they disobey his commands. In this way they are crippled—psychologically and spiritually—sometimes for life. Only too often they become unable to think for themselves, unable to develop. People generally do not realize what a disastrous effect their Christian upbringing, especially their belief in God, has had on them, until—sometimes—it is too late. They may realize it only when they try to break free from it, only when they try to become individuals. So for these reasons I do not think that Christianity can help us to correct the imbalance between the individual and the group. I do not think it can help us solve the problem of the individual. Christianity, I would say, has exacerbated the problem.

It might of course be said that the Christianity I have been talking about is not true Christianity. I must reply that this is the Christianity of history, the only Christianity that we really know. It is this Christianity which has oppressed us as individuals in the past, and which still oppresses us when it gets the opportunity today. It might be possible to imagine a better Christianity, but this Christianity would have to fulfil four conditions. First, it would have to entirely dissociate itself from what Aldous Huxley called, 'that savage, bronze-age literature' of the Old Testament. Secondly, it would have to give up the belief in God. (Some Christians have in fact already done this, as adroitly as they can, with their 'death of God' theology.) Thirdly, it would have to regard Christ as a teacher rather than as a Saviour. And fourthly, there would have to be an improvement in his teaching.

Until we have a Christianity of this kind we will just have to bring in Buddhism. We will just have to bring in something like the Friends of the Western Buddhist Order, a new spiritual movement which seeks to protect the individual from the group, which tries to correct the imbalance between the individual and the group, and which tries to solve the problem of the individual and the world today.

This spiritual movement will have to be a 'Buddhist' movement because Buddhism recognizes, as I think perhaps no other teaching does, the value of the individual. Buddhism shows the individual how to grow, how to become more and more of an individual; it allows him to develop in his own way. It also gives him the inspiring example of the Buddha and the support of the Sangha, or spiritual community, of other *individuals* with whom he is in direct personal contact.

All the same, it is not easy to be a Buddhist. It is certainly not easy to be a Western Buddhist. Historically speaking, at least, Buddhism is an Eastern religion. What the relationship is between Western Buddhists and Eastern Buddhism will be the subject of our next talk.

Western Buddhists and Eastern Buddhism

We will now be trying to understand the sense in which the FWBO is a specifically *Buddhist* movement. First of all, however, I must clear up two misunderstandings that could have arisen out of the previous talk.

The first arises in connection with the word 'individual'. You will recall that I spoke of our developing as an individual, as, even, a 'true individual'. But when I spoke in those terms I was not suggesting that we should become 'individual*ists*'. What, then, is the difference between an individual and an individualist? This distinction is quite crucial.

An individual is someone who has developed a higher level of what we call 'reflexive consciousness'. The individualist still 'shares' the consciousness of the group, the level of consciousness which manifests in all members of the group. The individualist has, we could say, a larger 'share' of this group consciousness than other members of the group, and therefore asserts his or her own interests at the expense of others in the group. The *individual* is therefore alienated from the group in what we may call a vertical direction, while the *individualist* is alienated from the group horizontally. The individualist is a sort of broken-off fragment of the group, reacting, even rebelling, against the group; he is the group writ small, a sort of one-man group—which is really a contradiction in terms, like a one-man band. The individual, on the other hand, has passed, or begun to pass, beyond the group, beyond group consciousness; he is no longer limited by group consciousness.

The second possible misunderstanding relates to the traditional Buddhist teaching of *anatta*, or *anatman*. *Anatta*, or *anatman*, literally means 'no self', or even 'non-self', depending upon the translation you prefer. But if you have read any sort of textbook on Buddhism you will know that Buddhism recognizes—as I've been insisting—the value of the individual, that it places the individual at the forefront of its teaching. It might therefore be objected that this recognition of the individual contradicts the teaching of 'no self'. Surely, the *anatta* teaching denies the very existence of a self, denies the existence of the individual, treats it as an illusion? What, then, are we to make of all this?

Where does the development of the individual fit in?

Fortunately, the difficulty is actually more apparent than real, because the *anatta* teaching does not really reject the existence of the self at all. Indeed, the Buddha specifically denied saying that the self does not exist. What the *anatta*, or *anatman*, teaching does deny is the existence of an *unchanging* self, and it does so for two reasons. It denies that there is an unchanging self—with the emphasis on the word 'unchanging'—because an unchanging self would contradict the Buddha's fundamental teaching of the impermanence—the changeful nature—of all conditioned things. Secondly, if the self were unchanging, the *development* of the self, the development of the individual, would be impossible. This would make the spiritual life, and thus Buddhism itself, impossible. However, we must be careful not to think that, because development is possible, there must be an unchanging individual who develops. What we have to realize is that the subject of the verb 'develop' is, in reality, a linguistic fiction.

We can now proceed to the meaning of the word 'Buddhist' in the name of our new spiritual movement, the Friends of the Western Buddhist Order. In what sense is the FWBO a Buddhist movement? Clearly, this very much depends on what we mean by 'Buddhist'—and that depends on what we mean by 'Buddhism'.

There are many, many different versions of Buddhism, and many interpretations. After all, the word 'Buddhism' itself represents an interpretation. Buddhism was not originally called Buddhism at all. It was certainly never called Buddhism in India, and it was certainly never called Buddhism by the Buddha. It was called the *Dharma* in Sanskrit, or *Dhamma* in Pali. And the word *Dharma*, or *Dhamma*, means Reality, or Truth; it means law, doctrine, or teaching. Or, one may say, it represents Reality or Truth as communicated in the form of a teaching from the Enlightened to the unenlightened mind. The originator of this Dharma, this vision of reality as a teaching, is, of course, Gautama the Buddha. He communicates to his followers a reality, a truth which he has personally experienced—the experience of which constitutes Enlightenment. Therefore, the Buddha is the best spokesman, the best interpreter, of Buddhism. So what does the Buddha himself say that the Dharma is? In this connection we can refer to an episode in the Pali scriptures, for the Buddha himself was once asked this very question, namely: 'What is your Dharma? What is your teaching?'

The person who asked this was Maha-Pajapati Gotami, the Buddha's aunt and foster-mother. She had brought him up since childhood, since the death of his mother when he was just a few days old. In later years Maha-Pajapati Gotami had not only become a follower of his teaching, but had 'gone forth', as we say, after hearing those teachings from his own lips. She had been so impressed by them that she had wanted to give up all her other interests, connections, and ties, so as to be able to devote her entire life to practising the Dharma. She had therefore gone forth, leaving her home, leaving her family, leaving her husband, leaving the city of Kapilavastu, and wandering from place to place, meditating and seeking to practise the Dharma.

At the time of our episode, Maha-Pajapati Gotami had passed a period of time without any direct contact with the Buddha, and so there was a certain amount of confusion in her mind. She wanted to practise the Dharma, but she was not quite sure what the Dharma was. This is not such an uncommon thing. Sometimes, at least, many of us may find ourselves in the position of wanting to practise the truth, without being quite sure, or even at all sure, what the truth actually is.

Although Maha-Pajapati Gotami was in contact with some of the Buddha's disciples and was able to ask them what it was that the Buddha taught, the interpretations they gave her were often very different; they each had their own point of view. In the end she decided to go and ask the Buddha himself what it was that he did fundamentally teach. She therefore made the journey to the place where the Buddha was staying and asked, point blank, as it were, 'What is your Dharma? How can we know what you actually do teach? What is the criterion?' Here is a translation of what, according to the tradition, the Buddha said to Maha-Pajapati Gotami on that occasion:

'Gotami, those things of which you know, "These things lead to passion, not to dispassion; to attachment, not to detachment; to amassing, not to dispersal; to ambition, not to modesty; to discontent, not to content; to association (association with the group, that is), not to seclusion (from the group); to idleness, not to energy; to luxury, not to frugality," of them, you can quite certainly decide. "This is not the Dharma, this is not the Vinaya, this is not the Master's teaching."

'But those things of which you know, "These things lead to dispassion, not to passion; to detachment, not to attachment; to dispersal, not to amassing; to modesty, not to ambition; to content, not to discontent; to seclusion (from the group), not to association (with the group); to energy, not to idleness; to frugality, not to luxury," of them you can quite certainly decide, "This is the Dharma, this is the Vinaya, this is the master's teaching."'

So here in the Buddha's own words is the criterion; this is the principle. The Dharma is

whatever contributes to the spiritual development of the individual. It is whatever the
individual finds, in his own experience, does
actually contribute to his own spiritual development.

Now in this passage, as in others, individuals
are clearly seen to be living, growing, and
developing. And in this connection we may also
remember the Buddha's 'vision' of humanity
immediately after his Enlightenment. At that
time, the Buddha was undecided as to whether
or not he should actually teach the truth he had
discovered. It was, he knew, something very
deep, very difficult and abstruse. But he eventually decided that he would go out and teach,
he would communicate the truth he had discovered to other beings. And at that moment, we
are told, he opened his eyes and looked out over
the world to see those living beings as a bed of
lotus flowers. It was as if he could see just a vast
bed of lotuses spreading in all directions, as far
as the eye could reach. This was humanity. This
was the human race. Some of these 'flowers'—
some of these people—were clearly sunk in the
mud. Others had risen just a little way out of it
and were struggling free. Others still had broken
out of the mud altogether and their heads were
rising above the surface of the water so that their
petals could open out to receive the light of the
sun.

This is how the Buddha saw humanity at that moment. He saw all beings as individuals, and he could see that they were all at different stages of development, all growing but needing the sunlight of the Dharma in order to grow and develop further.

In another passage, in the great Mahayana sutra called the '*Saddharma-pundarika*' or 'White Lotus' Sutra, there is another very beautiful comparison. Here, individuals are compared not just to lotuses emerging from the mud and slime, but to many different kinds of plants. They are compared to grass, trees, flowers, and shrubs, while the Buddha's teaching is compared to a great rain-cloud. During the winter and summer in India it is very hot and dry for many months. Everything becomes very withered and parched. But then, suddenly, at the beginning of the rainy season, a great black cloud arises in the midst of the sky. There is thunder, lightning, and then the rain falls, very heavily and very steadily, day in and day out, sometimes for weeks on end. And as it rains, everything grows. Everything that was so parched and dry becomes green again and starts springing up. All the leaves, all the grass, trees, flowers, and shrubs, start to grow again. And everything grows in its own way. The tree grows as a tree, the shrub grows as a shrub, the grass grows as grass, the flower grows as a flower; each grows in its own way. This is important to the Buddha's analogy, for the Dharma is just like that rain-cloud: it gives us just the nourishment we each need. It leads us from where it finds us, its starting point—so far as we are concerned—being where we are now, because everyone needs the Dharma in his or her own way.

This is also what we find the great Tibetan poet and mystic, Milarepa, saying in one of his songs: everybody needs the Dharma, but they need it in their own way. Here are just a few of the verses which he sang on a certain occasion:

Superior men have need of Dharma;
Without it, they are like eagles—
Even though perched on high,
They have but little meaning.

Average men have need of Dharma;
Without it, they are like tigers—
Though possessing greatest strength,
They are of little value.

Inferior men have need of Dharma;
Without it, they are like pedlar's asses—
Though they carry a big load,
It does them but little good.

Superior women need the Dharma;
Without it, they are like pictures on a wall—
Though they look pretty,
They have no use or meaning.

Average women need the Dharma;
Without it they are like little rats—

Though they are clever at getting food,
Their lives have but little meaning.

Inferior women need the Dharma;
Without it they are just like little vixens—
Though they be deft and cunning,
Their deeds have little value.

Old men have need of Dharma; without
It they are like decaying trees.
Growing youths the Dharma need;
Without it, they are like yoked bulls.
Young maidens need the Dharma; without
It they are but decorated cows.
All young people need the Dharma; without
It they are as blossoms shut within a shell.
All children need the Dharma; without it
They are as robbers possessed by demons.

Without the Dharma, all one
Does lacks meaning and purpose.
Those who want to live with meaning
Should practise the Buddha's teaching.

Milarepa's song makes it clear that the meaning
and purpose of life for the individual is to grow,
is to rise to a higher level of consciousness, and
that this is what the Dharma helps us to do. The
Dharma is whatever helps us to rise from
wherever we are now, and from whatever we
are now. The Dharma is therefore defined as
whatever contributes to the development of the
individual. That is the criterion.

This may sound rather broad and general, but it is not really so. The Dharma—the Buddha's teaching—is embodied in a number of actual spiritual practices. This is made clear in another episode from the Pali scriptures. In this particular episode we are reminded that there were a number of spiritual teachers in India during the Buddha's time. One of the best known of these was Nigantha Nataputta, as he is called in the Pali texts, who is usually identified with Mahavira, the founder of Jainism. Nigantha Nataputta died shortly before the Buddha, and after his death his monk followers split into two factions. These factions disagreed so vehemently about what their master had taught that they almost came to blows. Ananda, who seems to have been something of a gossip, told the Buddha about this, adding that he hoped there would be no such disputes after the Buddha himself had gone.

The Buddha's replied that such a thing would be impossible. He was confident that there were not even two monks among his followers who would describe his teachings discordantly. He then reminded Ananda what those teachings were. There were the four foundations of mindfulness: mindfulness of the body, of the feelings, thoughts, and of Reality. There were the four 'right efforts': the effort to prevent the arising of unskilful mental states that have not arisen; the effort to abandon unskilful mental states that have arisen; the effort to develop skilful mental states that have not arisen; and the effort to maintain in existence those skilful mental states that have already arisen. He reminded Ananda about the four bases of success, the five spiritual faculties, the five powers, the seven factors of Enlightenment, the Noble Eightfold Path, ... All these things constituted the Dharma that he had taught and about which he was confident there would be no dispute after his death even between two of his disciples.

The immediately noticeable thing about this list of teachings is that they are all practical. They are all actual *practices*. There is nothing theoretical here; the Buddha says nothing about Nirvana, nothing about *Sunyata*, nothing about the mind. He does not even mention 'dependent origination'. It is as if he is saying that the teachings he has given his disciples are all practical teachings and cannot therefore really be described differently by different people. After all, practical teachings involve actual practice and so the experience would be the same for all who practised. It is much the same in ordinary life; we may disagree about theory, but we do not very often disagree about practice. We may disagree, for example, about the nature of electricity, but we are unlikely to disagree about how to mend a fuse. Similarly, the Buddha's disciples might disagree about theoretical teachings, but they could hardly disagree about practical teachings, provided of course that they had actually practised them. So the Dharma is embodied primarily in spiritual practices, in things that you actually do.

There is another interesting point which arises in connection with this episode. Despite the Buddha's answer, Ananda was not satisfied. He now said, 'Well, even though they may all agree about the teaching, there might still be disputes about livelihood, or there might be disputes about the code of rules (Pali: *pati-mokkha*, the hundred-and-fifty rules observed by the monks, still observed in many cases)'. The Buddha's reply to this was very important. A dispute over livelihood, or a dispute over the code of rules, he said, would be a 'trifling matter'. It is only disputes over the path, or disputes over the way of practice, that would be disastrous.

Now that we have briefly seen what is meant by Buddhism, we can begin to see in what sense the FWBO is a Buddhist movement. It is a Buddhist movement first of all in the sense that it is concerned with the individual. Buddhism values the individual in a way that no other teaching does. And Buddhism is simply whatever helps that individual to grow, whatever helps him or her to develop from lower to higher levels of being and consciousness. At the same time, the Dharma does not represent just a vague general principle of growth; it is embodied in specific spiritual practices.

This last point, however, may leave some people troubled by the following question: If Buddhism is whatever contributes to the development of the individual, does it have to be confined only to what is labelled as 'Buddhism'? Could one not say that whatever contributes to the development of the individual is in fact Buddhism, or at least part of Buddhism?

There are two things that I should perhaps mention in this connection. Some people in the FWBO get a great deal of inspiration from certain Western poets and philosophers, an inspiration which helps them in their spiritual life as Buddhists. I can think of Goethe, of Blake, of Schopenhauer, Nietzsche, Plato, D.H. Lawrence, and Shelley. (Quite a miscellaneous collection, you might think!) Yet other Friends derive inspiration from Western classical music, especially from that of Bach, Beethoven, and Mozart. This is quite in order, and one could certainly count such inspiration as part of Buddhism in the wider sense.

When I say this, however, I am not suggesting that people like Goethe, Blake, and so on—great as they were—were as Enlightened as the Buddha. I am not saying that their poetry or their philosophy or their music can take us as far as can the Dharma—that is to say, the Dharma in the narrower sense. But at present we have to recognize that most people in the FWBO are still at a quite elementary stage in their spiritual life, and they need the help which is appropriate to that stage. Perhaps I should quote the words of sGampopa, the great Tibetan mystic, when he says, 'The greatest benefactor is a spiritual friend in the form of an ordinary human being.' An *'ordinary' human being* is ordinary, in this instance, when compared to the Buddhas and the Bodhisattvas. By that standard, even Goethe and Blake were ordinary.

Secondly, regardless of the inspiration one may get from these other sources, the principal source of inspiration for the FWBO is nonetheless the Buddha and his teachings. It is from there that we get our idea of what constitutes development; it is from there that we get our ideal of human Enlightenment. So whatever help we get from other sources must be in accordance with that, in harmony with that, and must lead us in the direction of human Enlightenment. This, then, is why we call ourselves the Friends of the Western *Buddhist* Order, rather than something else.

The FWBO is, as we have already seen, a Western spiritual movement, a Western spiritual phenomenon. It seeks to practise Buddhism under the conditions of modern Western civilization, which is a secularized and industrialized civilization. But, historically speaking at least, Buddhism is an Eastern religion. It originated in India, and for two-thousand-five-hundred years it has been virtually confined to the East. It is only quite recently, in the course of the last hundred years in fact, that it has become known in the West at all. So what is the relation between Western Buddhists and Eastern Buddhism?

In attempting to answer this question, the first thing that has to be said is that there is no such thing as Eastern Buddhism. What we actually have is a number of Eastern Buddhisms, in the plural. Broadly speaking there are four of these now extant in the Eastern Buddhist world. There is South-East Asian Buddhism, Chinese Buddhism, Japanese Buddhism, and Tibetan Buddhism.

South-East Asian Buddhism is found in Sri Lanka, Burma, Thailand, and in Cambodia—as well as, here and there, in Singapore and Malaysia. This form of Buddhism belongs to the Theravada school, whose scriptures are contained in the Pali Tipitaka—in some forty-five volumes in the Royal Thai edition.

Chinese Buddhism is found mainly in China, Taiwan, Korea, Vietnam, and, again, in parts of Singapore and Malaysia. (I am of course ignoring recent political developments which have certainly altered the situation.) Chinese Buddhism belongs to what we may call 'general', or non-sectarian, Mahayana, and its scriptures are contained in the *Tsa-tsan*, or 'Three Treasuries', corresponding to the Tipitaka, in fifty-five volumes. These volumes are very much bigger than the volumes of the Pali Tipitaka. In this particular collection there are no less than 1,662 independent works, a few of which are almost as long as the Christian Bible.

Japanese Buddhism is found, of course, in Japan, but also in Hawaii, and among Japanese immigrants in mainland USA. It comprises various schools of what may be described as 'sectarian' Mahayana. The best known of these are Zen and Shin. There are also various modern schools developed even in the present century. The scriptures of Japanese Buddhism are the Chinese Tsa-tsan plus various Japanese works according to sect—which may in practice sometimes displace the Tsa-tsan.

Tibetan Buddhism is found in Tibet, Mongolia, Sikkim, Bhutan, Ladakh, parts of China, and even in parts of the USSR. It consists of four main traditions, all of which follow all three of the *yanas*—that is, Hinayana, Mahayana, and Vajrayana. The differences between these four traditions occur mainly in respect of Vajrayana—that is to say Tantric—lineages. Their scriptures are all contained in the Kangyur, which means the 'Buddha-word', in 100 or 108 (according to the edition) xylographed volumes, plus special collections like the *Rinchen-Terma* for the Nyingmapas, or the *Milarepa Kabum* in the case of the Kagyupas.

These are the four extant Eastern schools of Buddhism. There are many intermediate forms, and sub-forms, and sub-sub-forms, but for the sake of simplicity I have ignored them. For practical purposes Western Buddhists find themselves confronted by four Eastern Buddhisms rather than by just one monolithic Eastern Buddhism with complementary unitary features.

Perhaps I could just add here that they do not find themselves confronted by an Eastern mind, or by an Eastern psychology either. Some writers speak of the Western mind and the Eastern mind as though they were two completely different minds, and it is suggested that it is very difficult for the Eastern mind to understand the Western mind, and vice versa. Buddhism of course is supposed to be a product of the Eastern mind, which is why, we are sometimes told, it is difficult for Westerners to understand Buddhism. Speaking from experience, however, I have found no evidence for any such belief. Wherever I went during my twenty years in the East, whether I was associating with Indians, Tibetans, Mongolians, Thais, or Sinhalese—or even Europeans, I found that I could understand them, and they could understand me. Buddhism is admittedly difficult to understand, but not because it is a product of the 'Eastern mind'. It is difficult to understand because it is a product of the *Enlightened* mind, a mind which transcends the conditionings of both the East and the West.

Another popular myth which I might as well mention in this connection it is that there is a 'spiritual' East, and a 'materialistic' West. This really is another myth. The West is no more materialistic than the East. One might say that the West is simply more 'successful' in its pursuit of materialism.

However, to return to the theme of Western Buddhists and the four Eastern Buddhisms, these four Eastern Buddhisms are differentiated from each other in two main ways. They are differentiated, first of all, according to the doctrinal school of Buddhism to which they belong. Secondly, they are differentiated according to the regional or national culture with which they are associated.

From a practical point of view, at least, the second of these is probably the more important since, as a consequence, the Buddhism that most people come across in the West, whether in content or in practice, is not really Buddhism. We could even say that many Western Buddhists never really encounter Buddhism at all. What they encounter is a particular school or sub-school of Buddhism associated with a particular national or regional culture. They may encounter the Theravada, for instance, which is associated with South-East Asian—specifically Sinhalese—culture. Or they may encounter Zen, which is associated with Japanese culture, and so on.

But the situation is even more complicated than that. Buddhism arose in India, a country with a very rich and ancient culture. From its very beginning, from the moment it emerged from the Buddha's mouth, so to speak, Buddhism was associated with Indian culture, indeed with Indian cultures, because in the course of the fifteen hundred years during which Buddhism was alive in India, Indian culture went through several different phases of development, each with very strongly marked characteristics.

When Buddhism went on from India to China, what actually 'went' was Buddhism plus Indian culture. Then, in China, Buddhism assumed certain Chinese cultural characteristics before going on to Japan. In Japan, of course, Buddhism assumed certain Japanese characteristics. So today, Japanese Buddhism consists of Buddhism plus Indian culture plus Chinese culture plus Japanese culture. *That* is the Buddhism which is coming to the United States of America, to Britain, to Australia, and so on. Sometimes, of course, the Buddhism succeeds in penetrating all those layers of culture which are superimposed upon it, but sometimes it does not.

Confronted by these different Eastern Buddhisms, the first thing that the Western Buddhist has to do is learn to distinguish what is really Buddhism from what is actually South-East Asian, or Chinese, or Japanese, or Tibetan, or even Indian culture. It is not that there is anything wrong with any of those cultures; they are often very beautiful indeed. But they are not the same thing as Buddhism, not the same thing as the Dharma. When we say that the FWBO is a Buddhist spiritual movement we do not mean that we have adopted some particular form of Eastern culture—though, at the same time, this does not necessarily mean that we reject Eastern Buddhist culture. Some of that culture does express the spirit of Buddhism. One might think, for example, of the Japanese art of flower arrangement—this surely expresses something the spirit of Buddhism. In the FWBO we are very happy to adopt this kind of Eastern culture, but we adopt it because it can be approached as an expression of *Buddhism*, because it helps us in our spiritual development, and not just because it is Eastern.

However, some Western Buddhists are unable to make this distinction between Buddhism and Eastern culture. They think that they are attracted by Buddhism when in reality they are attracted to an exotic oriental culture. Sometimes they think that they are trying to be Buddhists when in reality they are just trying to copy Indians, Japanese, or Tibetans—or at least to look like them. This is quite harmless of course. There is no harm in dressing up as an Indian, or pretending to be Japanese, or imagining that you are a Tibetan. It is quite harmless— except to the extent that it represents an alienation from your own culture. But it has nothing to do with actually being a Buddhist.

In some parts of the West we now have a very strange situation indeed. All four of the main Eastern Buddhisms have now been introduced. They have their Western followers, all of whom are supposedly Buddhists; but because they follow different Eastern cultures they are unable to live together or to practise Buddhism together.

I remember an example of this sort of thing from the very early days of the FWBO. Not far from London lived a group of English Zen Buddhists. They decided that they would like to join one of our FWBO communities, and, after some discussion, we agreed—even though I had my own misgivings. Almost as soon as they had moved in, a difficulty arose: they refused to join in the puja—that is, the evening devotions. The reason for this was that our puja was recited in Pali and English, and their guru (who was, incidentally, an English woman who had spent some time in Japan) had told them that they should do their puja only in Japanese. So while some members of the community performed their puja in English and Pali these English Zen

Buddhists waited outside the shrine-room; they would not even sit in the room and listen.

Another example comes to mind in connection with this same guru. Japanese culture is what sociologists call a 'shame culture'. In Japanese culture shame is used as a technique of social control. (Our Western Christian culture is probably a 'guilt culture'.) In traditional Japanese society, when a young person misbehaves, an older person will proceed to imitate him—but greatly exaggerating the misdemeanour. If the young person has been noisy, the older person will be four or five times as noisy. If he has slammed a door the older person must go and slam it three or four times very, very loudly. The young person then feels ashamed; he realizes that he has been corrected and desists from that particular misbehaviour out of shame. At some stage this technique of control through shame was transferred to the Japanese Zen temple. If the disciple misbehaved the master would imitate him. If the disciple slouched during meditation the master would immediately slouch right over; the disciple would notice, feel ashamed, pull himself up straight, and in that way he would learn. The technique was known as 'mirroring'.

Now this English/Japanese Zen guru happened to pass through London some years ago. It seems that she did not very much like what some of the English Buddhists, who had not been to Japan, were doing. So she started mirroring them. Her head monk, an American who was accompanying her, started mirroring them as well. For example, thinking that English Buddhists ate far too much while on retreat, he started mirroring them, and took a second helping of everything, just to them show how greedy they were. However, the English Buddhists, not being Japanese, did not understand what was going on. They thought the poor fellow must be hungry, and gave him a third helping of everything. The guru, I heard, was quite annoyed. She said that English Buddhists were stupid because they could not appreciate her mirroring technique. But really it was she who could not understand that mirroring was part of Japanese culture; it had nothing to do with Buddhism, and it was not appropriate in the West.

The FWBO is definitely a Buddhist spiritual movement. But it does not confuse Buddhism with any of its Eastern cultural forms. In the same way, the FWBO does not identify itself exclusively with any particular sect or school of Buddhism, not with the Hinayana, nor with the Mahayana, nor with the Vajrayana, nor with the Theravada, nor with Zen, Shin, or the Nyingmapas. It is just *Buddhist*. At the same time it does not reject any of the sects or schools that have arisen in the course of the long history of Buddhism. It appreciates them all and seeks to learn from them all, taking from them whatever it can find that contributes to the spiritual development of the individual in the West. As regards meditation practice, for instance, we teach the 'mindfulness of breathing', and the *metta bhavana*, the 'development of universal loving kindness', which are taken from the Theravada tradition. We recite the Sevenfold Puja—which comes from the Indian Mahayana tradition. We chant mantras which come from the Tibetan tradition. And then of course there is our emphasis on the importance of work in the spiritual life, which is a characteristically Zen emphasis. Naturally, we also have certain emphases which are not to be found in any extant form of Buddhism: for example, our emphasis on Right Livelihood, on Going for Refuge, and on 'more and more of less and less'.

Although we take what we need from all these sources, our attitude is not one of eclecticism. Eclecticism is a purely intellectual attitude. We may take different things from different forms of Buddhism, but we take them according to our actual spiritual needs, rather than in accordance with any preconceived intellectual ideas. We take whatever will help us *grow* under the conditions of Western life.

We adopt much the same sort of attitude towards the Buddhist scriptures. There are an enormous number of these, as you have already gathered, and it would be impossible to study them all. Actually, we are not in fact meant to;

they represent the same basic teachings in varying degrees of expansion and contraction. Instead, we read and study intensively whatever we find most helpful to us in the spiritual life. Our study texts are therefore drawn from all sources: from Pali, Sanskrit, Chinese, and Tibetan. Among others we study the *Udana*, which is found in the Pali Tipitaka, the *Bodhicaryavatara*, which is a Sanskrit Mahayana work compiled in India, *Dhyana for Beginners*, which is based on the lectures of a Chinese master, *The Jewel Ornament of Liberation*, the work of a Tibetan master, and *The Songs of Milarepa*, the teachings of one of the greatest Tantric yogins of the Buddhist tradition.

We should now be able to see the nature of the relation between Western Buddhists—or at least Western Buddhists in the FWBO—and the various Eastern Buddhisms. But another question might arise at this point. If, as we have seen, the FWBO does not follow Eastern Buddhism as such, is it then trying to create a *distinctively* Western Buddhism? Is it trying to express Buddhism in terms of Western culture?

The answer is both yes and no, and depends very much on what one actually understands by Western culture. As we have already seen, the FWBO is not 'against' Western culture as such: there are certain affinities between the works of the great Western poets, philosophers, and musicians, and certain aspects of Buddhism. But this is not true of Western culture as a whole—in which must be included our social and economic systems. Western culture, as it stands as a whole, is quite incompatible with Buddhism and there can be no question of our seeking to express Buddhism in terms of that culture. It is a question, rather, of Western Buddhism finding expression in a *new* Western culture, a culture which would in its own way, on its own level, help people to develop, if not spiritually then at least psychologically. In creating that culture we would of course keep the best elements of the traditional Western culture, but a lot would have to go.

So far as the FWBO is concerned there is no question of our simply finding a little place for ourselves in the contemporary Western world without trying to change that world. It is not just a question of studying Buddhism and then doing what everybody else does in all practical matters, and living as everybody else lives. This is one of the points that makes the FWBO a new Buddhist movement: it is not content just to inhabit a little niche.

The FWBO was founded in 1967. In those days there were two different kinds of Buddhist group in England. Firstly, there were groups run by Eastern Buddhists—Sinhalese Buddhists, Tibetans, Thais, and so on—who had come here for that purpose. They all propagated Buddhism in a particular Eastern cultural form or setting—

sometimes, unfortunately, propagating Eastern culture rather than Buddhism. Secondly, there were groups run by English Buddhists. These tended simply to study Buddhism: to read books, listen to lectures, and maybe in some cases practise a little meditation. I remember, for instance, being told on my return to London in 1964 that English Buddhists were not able to practise more than five minutes meditation at a time, and that I was on no account to try to give them more! That was the standard in those days. People tended simply to study Buddhism, read lots and lots of books about Buddhism, hear lots and lots of lectures about Buddhism, and in some cases practise a very little meditation. But in their everyday life they lived like everybody else, with the same social, economic, and political ideas and ideals as the non-Buddhists (of their own class, that is). Being a Buddhist made no difference in any of these areas; they rarely even practised Right Livelihood, and didn't even think of practising it. Furthermore, although they studied Buddhism, they rarely studied it from the Buddhist point of view. In many cases they did not even think of themselves as Buddhists. They studied Buddhism, strange as it may sound, from the Christian point of view, or at least with unconscious Christian conditioning.

Very recently a group of students from the Open University, along with their tutor, paid a visit to the London Buddhist Centre. During the course of their visit it emerged that both the students and their tutor—who was a Methodist minister—had some very strange ideas about Buddhism. According to the textbook for their course on Buddhism—which had been written by a Belgian Jesuit priest—the Theravada was annihilationist, the Mahayana was corrupt and degenerate, and the Vajrayana was just magical nonsense. No wonder they were confused!

This is the sort of thing which is still going on in academic circles. But when I returned to England in 1964, and again in 1967, things were almost as bad in ostensibly Buddhist circles. English Buddhists, for instance, who studied the Pali scriptures, not only said that the Pali scriptures were the word of the Buddha, but that *only those scriptures* were the word of the Buddha, and that other Buddhist scriptures were not the word of the Buddha at all. Naturally, one was therefore not allowed to question anything that was recorded in the Pali scriptures. After all, the Buddha was Enlightened and the Buddha had uttered every word that was found in them. These English Buddhists were in fact Pali fundamentalists! They adopted towards the Pali scriptures the same sort of attitude that Christian, especially Protestant, fundamentalists adopt towards the Bible. It was as if they had transferred their Christian attitudes from

Christianity to Buddhism without making any real change at all.

The FWBO, I hope, adopts a different attitude. It tries to see Buddhism from the Buddhist point of view. And it seeks to create a new Western civilization and culture, one which will express Buddhist spiritual values, one which will help the individual to develop instead of hindering him or her, and one which will provide the basis for a spiritual community and a new society.

We have now seen that the FWBO is a Buddhist movement in the sense that it is concerned with the individual. We have seen that Buddhism, according to the Buddha, is whatever helps the individual to grow. We have further seen that Buddhism is not exclusively limited to whatever is labelled as 'Buddhism'. At the same time we have seen that Buddhism is not just a vague and general principle of growth, but is embodied in specific spiritual principles and practices. We have also seen that the FWBO distinguishes sharply between Buddhism and Eastern Buddhist culture, and that it is not limited to any sectarian form of Buddhism but appreciates and seeks to learn from—and gain inspiration from—all forms of Buddhism without exception. We have seen too that it seeks to create a new Western culture based on genuine Buddhist values, and that it seeks to see Buddhism in terms of Buddhism—that is to say in terms of the individual evolving in the direction of what we can only call Enlightenment.

Commitment and spiritual community

In order to explain the sense in which the Friends of the Western Buddhist Order is based on an *Order*, and the sense in which it is a movement of Friends, I need to offer a little in the way of autobiography. This will help me to explain what it was that led me to start an Order and a movement of friends, rather than just another Buddhist organization of the usual type.

Before returning to England in 1964 I spent altogether twenty years in the East. I spent most of those years in India, initially as a sort of Hindu-Buddhist ascetic, wandering in southern India, meditating, studying, meeting famous teachers, and so on (a part of that story is related in my volume of memoirs, *The Thousand Petalled Lotus*). I then spent a year in Benares, studying Pali, Abhidhamma, and logic. Finally, I spent fourteen years in the foothills of the Himalayas in a place called Kalimpong, about four thousand feet above sea level, sandwiched between Nepal to the west, Bhutan to the east, Sikkim to the north, and, beyond Sikkim of course, Tibet.

Although I kept in touch with various Indian Buddhist organizations during all this time, I did not join any of them. I kept in touch, but I never joined. It was as if some instinct was holding me back. One organization with which I maintained particular contact was quite an old one. It was also fairly well known, for in its day it had done a lot of good work for Buddhism in India. Now I had not been in touch with this organization for very long before I began to feel quite dissatisfied with it. My dealings, both by letter and also from time to time in person, were mainly with the governing body, which, including office bearers, consisted of about forty people. Most of them, I soon discovered, were not Buddhists. This rather surprised me. In those days I was a little inexperienced, not to say naïve, and so was rather shocked to find that the majority of the members of the governing body of a prominent Buddhist organization were not even Buddhists.

At first I felt that this must be all right, that these people must be genuinely sympathetic to Buddhism even though they were not actually Buddhists. But in time I found that this was not the case either. Very much to my dismay I discovered that some members of the governing body had no sympathy with Buddhism at all. In some cases they were actually hostile to it, even though they were running the organization's affairs.

Naturally enough, I began to wonder how this had happened, and came to realize that these people were running the affairs of the organization quite simply because they had been *elected* to its governing body. And how had they been elected? They had been elected at an annual general meeting. And how had they come to be present at that annual general meeting? They were there because they were paid-up members of the organization. How had they become members of that organization? Simply by paying a subscription. This, then, seemed to me to be at the root of the trouble: these people had got where they were simply by paying a small sum of money, plus, of course, a bit of string pulling. It seemed a very strange way to run a Buddhist organization; no wonder it was not functioning very well.

You might wonder why it was that people who were not really sympathetic to Buddhism should take the time and trouble to run the affairs of a Buddhist organization. After many years of experience I now know that there are some people who like to belong to organizations, who like to get on to governing bodies and managing committees, whether religious, political, civic, or social. It gives them a feeling of power. They just like to run things and they don't mind very much what it is that they are running.

In the case of this particular Buddhist organization there was yet another factor at work. The organization was quite well known, and used to organize big public meetings, to celebrate the Buddha's birthday for instance. In India public meetings are really very big; you can get a hundred thousand people, even five hundred thousand people, coming along. That was the kind of public meeting that this particular organization used to organize, and of course famous politicians and prominent businessmen would be invited to preside over them, so that if you were a member of the governing body you would be sitting up on the platform with all these people, basking in their reflected glory. Naturally you would get to know them, and getting to know these celebrities would be very useful to you in your own political or business life. You might even get some favour in that way, because in India after all, everything is done by personal influence. So, as you can perhaps imagine, what I saw in India made me rather disillusioned with Buddhist organizations.

When I returned to England after twenty years in the East I thought that things would be different. However, as I spent my first two years working with existing Buddhist organizations, mainly in London, I must admit that I found things pretty much the same—only on a very much smaller scale. Again there were plenty of non-Buddhists having quite a big say in the running of Buddhist organizations, and consequently those organizations too were not functioning very well, at least from a Buddhist point of view.

I therefore decided that something had to be done. A new Buddhist organization would have to be started, an organization which would not be an organization. I had already decided to remain in England because I saw that in England—in fact in the West generally—there was scope for a genuinely Buddhist movement, but I now felt the need to start a new one, indeed, a new kind of Buddhist movement altogether. This was of course what was eventually started as the FWBO and the WBO.

It is not as easy to start up something new, not as easy to start a new spiritual movement, as one might think. It is said that a young clergyman once paid a visit to Voltaire, the great French writer and thinker. This clergyman's faith in the Church and Christianity was crumbling and he thought it would be a good idea to start a new religion. So when he was in the presence of the great sage of his time he asked, 'What should I do in order to start a new religion?' Voltaire replied, 'It is really very easy; you just have to do two things. First of all you must get yourself crucified, and then you must rise from the dead.'

It is not as easy to start a new religion as you might think. It is not very easy even to start a new spiritual movement. But although it may not be at all clear at first what *has* to be done, I think I can say that it is usually quite clear how things are *not* to be done. And one thing that was clear to me was that Buddhist organizations could not be run by non-Buddhists. They could not be run simply by people who were good at running things, however efficiently they might do it. And they certainly couldn't be run by people who were merely after power and influence, or name and fame. A Buddhist spiritual movement could be run only by real Buddhists, by those who were actually *committed* to Buddhism and who actually practised the Buddha's teachings, not by those who had merely an intellectual interest in it. Strangely enough, this was not generally realized at the time. People seemed to think that a spiritual movement could be run by people who were not themselves spiritually motivated.

But my view of things presented some important questions. How was one to know who was spiritually motivated? How could one know who was a Buddhist? What in fact *was* a Buddhist? What was the criterion? Eventually, the answer became clear. In a way I had known it all along, but now I saw it in a new light. A Buddhist is one who 'goes for Refuge' to the Buddha, the Dharma, and the Sangha, is one who *commits* himself to the Buddha, the Dharma, and the Sangha, and who commits himself to them totally, with body, speech, and mind.

There are many stories to illustrate what this means in the ancient Buddhist scriptures. When we read those scriptures, especially the Pali scriptures, we encounter the Buddha as he wanders from place to place, begging his food as he goes. In the course of his wanderings, he might meet somebody under a tree, or in a village, and the two of them get into a conversation. Maybe it's a Brahmin priest, or a farmer, or a well-to-do merchant; or a young man about town. Maybe it's a wandering ascetic, maybe it's a housewife, maybe it's a prince, … but in one way or another they get talking.

Sooner or later, this person asks the Buddha a question, perhaps about the meaning of life, or about his teaching, or about what happens after death. The Buddha might reply at considerable length, giving a detailed discourse, or he might reply in just a few words. If he is very inspired he might reply in verse, 'breathing out' what is called an *Udana*. He might even give one of his famous 'lion roars', a full and frank, almost defiant, declaration of his great spiritual experience and the path that he teaches; or he might reply with complete silence—a wordless communication that says so much more than words. But whatever the Buddha says or does not say, if the listener is receptive, the result is the same. He or she feels deeply affected, deeply moved, deeply stirred. They are so stirred, so thrilled, in fact, that their hair might stand on end, or they might shed tears, or be seized by a violent fit of trembling. They feel as if they are seeing a great light; they have a tremendous sense of emancipation; they feel as if a great burden has been lifted from their back, or as though they have been suddenly let out of prison. At such a moment, the listener feels spiritually reborn. And at that extraordinary turning point they respond to the Buddha and to the Dharma with a cry that breaks spontaneously from their lips. According to those ancient Pali texts, they say; *'Buddham saranam gacchami, Dhammam saranam gacchami, Sangham saranam gacchami,'* which means, 'To the Buddha for Refuge I go, to the Dharma for Refuge I go, to the Sangha for Refuge I go.' This is their response: they go for Refuge, commit themselves, because the Buddha has shown them a vision of inner truth, of existence, of life itself in all its depth and complexity. This vision is so great that all one can do is give oneself to it completely, live for it, and if necessary die for it.

But what does one actually mean when one says, 'To the Buddha for Refuge I go; to the Dharma for Refuge I go; to the Sangha for Refuge I go'? The English word 'refuge' is not very satisfactory. It is a literal translation of the Pali and Sanskrit word *sarana*, but does not give its real meaning. There is certainly no question of running away from anything when one goes for Refuge, no question of taking shelter with anyone. Going for Refuge really means commitment: committing oneself to the Buddha, committing oneself to the Dharma, committing oneself to the Sangha. So what does this mean?

Committing oneself to the Buddha does not mean handing oneself over to the Buddha or blindly obeying the Buddha. It means taking the Buddha as one's ideal, taking *Buddhahood* as an ideal. The historical Buddha, Gautama, was a human being. By his own human efforts he developed higher and ever higher states of being, states that eventually culminated in what we call 'Enlightenment', the highest conceivable state of moral and spiritual perfection, a state of supreme wisdom, of infinite compassion, and absolute purity. We too are human beings; we too, therefore, according to Buddhism, are capable of developing higher and higher states of being and consciousness. We too are capable of gaining Enlightenment. This is what committing oneself to the Buddha means. It means recognizing the Buddha as the living embodiment of the highest conceivable state of human perfection. It means recognizing Buddhahood as a practical ideal for all human beings, and actually devoting all one's energies towards the realization of that ideal.

What is meant by 'committing oneself to the Dharma'? The Dharma is the teaching of the Buddha, and it is concerned mainly with two things: with the goal of Enlightenment, or Buddhahood, and with the path leading to that state. Committing oneself to the Dharma therefore means actually following the path in order to realize the goal. The path consists of several steps and stages which are variously enumerated according to the particular point of view adopted. One popular enumeration of the stages of the path is that of the three stages of morality, meditation, and wisdom. Another enumeration is that of the Noble Eightfold Path. This is not really a path of eight stages, as is generally thought, but a path of two stages: a stage of vision and a stage of transformation. The stage of vision represents an actual vision of the goal—not just a theoretical idea but an actual spiritual experience—and the stage of transformation represents the gradual transformation of all aspects of one's being, from the highest to the lowest, in accordance with that vision. There is also the path of the six perfections—of generosity, morality, patience, vigour, meditation, and wisdom. So committing oneself to the Dharma means following the path in any of these various ways. It means committing oneself to the process of one's development as an individual by whatsoever means.

The Sangha is the spiritual community—that is, the community of the spiritually committed. The Dharma, as we have seen, is a path which consists of various steps and stages. Naturally, different individuals are on different steps and at different stages. Some are more advanced than we are, some are less advanced, and some are equally advanced. What, then, is our attitude towards these people? We reverence those who are more advanced, we are receptive to their spiritual influence, and assist them in their spiritual work. We help those who are less advanced than we are, giving advice and moral support as and when we can. And we enjoy spiritual friendship with those who are as advanced as ourselves. Indeed, we can enjoy spiritual fellowship with all members of the sangha in different ways and in differing degrees. This is what we mean by committing ourselves to the Sangha.

Certainly each individual must develop for him- or herself, by his or her own efforts, but we will develop more easily and more enjoyably if we do so in spiritual fellowship with others. We could even say that spiritual fellowship is necessary to individual development. In the spiritual community all help each, and each helps all. In the end, all narrow, pseudo-religious individualism is transcended, there is only a spiritual community of individuals who are, as it were, transparent to each other, individuals through whom the light of Enlightenment shines.

So this is how one can know who is a Buddhist. A Buddhist is one who goes for Refuge in response to the Buddha and his teaching. A Buddhist is one who gives him- or herself to the Buddha and the Dharma and the Sangha. This was the criterion in the Buddha's day 2,500 years ago, and it remains the criterion today.

I had now come to see that a Buddhist organization could be run only by Buddhists, which meant that it could be run only by those who had committed themselves wholeheartedly to the Buddha, the Dharma, and the Sangha. But another thing that then became clear was that a Buddhist organization run by committed Buddhists would no longer be an organization in the ordinary sense of the word. It would be a spiritual movement. In fact it would be what we call a 'spiritual community', an association of committed individuals, freely working together for a common spiritual end.

We can now begin to see in what sense the FWBO is based around an 'Order', can begin to see, perhaps, what led me to start an Order rather than yet another Buddhist organization of the usual type. An Order consists of those who have been ordained. In Buddhist terms 'ordination' means giving full formal expression, in 'concrete' form, to one's commitment to the Buddha, the Dharma, and the Sangha, and having that commitment recognized by others already committed. One can join an organization by paying the required subscription, but one can be received into an Order only by way of ordination, only by committing oneself. This was the basis on which our new Buddhist movement was founded, the basis of commitment and spiritual community, or, in more traditional Buddhist language, of 'Going for Refuge' and 'Sangha'. But if this was the only basis on which it could be founded, you might therefore wonder why it had taken me such a long time to see it. You might also wonder why nobody else had thought in terms of commitment and spiritual community, why nobody else, in recent times at least, had started an Order instead of yet another Buddhist organization. So far as I can see there are three reasons for this, and I will give a brief account of them so as to offer a clearer idea of the difference between a spiritual community and a religious organization.

The first of these reasons is what I can only describe as inertia and force of habit. Buddhism started to become known in the West, including Westernized India, not much more than a hundred years ago. This was a time when the frontiers of knowledge, and especially of scientific knowledge, were expanding rapidly. Societies were set up at that time for the study of all sorts of things, and it was inevitable that sooner or later there should be societies devoted to the study of Buddhism and the publication of Buddhist texts. This was quite all right, so long as the approach remained purely scientific, purely academic. At this stage I am not questioning the validity of the scientific approach to spiritual traditions, but such an approach is no longer suitable when we are concerned with Buddhism in a more practical, spiritual, even existential way. Unfortunately people did not realize that a new kind of approach was required and assumed that an organization devoted to the practice and spread of Buddhism could have the same structure as an organization devoted to its scientific study. Not only that, the prominent people within those old Buddhist organizations were quite satisfied with things as they were since the existing set-up gave them a certain amount of power and authority which they did not want to relinquish.

The two other reasons are more traditional. The first of these was what we could call the 'devaluation' of the Going for Refuge. Buddhism has a long history. In the course of a thousand years Buddhism spread over practically the whole of Asia, and millions of people became Buddhists, millions of people committed themselves to the Buddha, the Dharma, and the Sangha. So far so good. But as time went by people started reciting the words, *'Buddham saranam gacchami'*, and so on, out of habit, or simply because their parents or their grandparents had recited them. They were not real Buddhists; they were not really committed to the ideals of Buddhism. Such people sometimes regard themselves as 'born Buddhists', as though such a thing were not a contradiction in terms. This is the situation today in the Buddhist countries of Asia to a great extent. The Going for Refuge is no longer regarded as an expression of genuine, individual spiritual commitment, but has become a recitation which simply shows that one belongs to a particular social or cultural group.

I had plenty of personal experience of this sort of thing while I was in India. I found Sinhalese, Thai, Burmese, and Indian Buddhists reciting the Refuges and the precepts on all sorts of occasions—at big public meetings, at weddings, at funerals.... People would recite the words, and yet nobody bothered about their significance. They recited the refuges and precepts just to show they were good Buddhists or they were respectable citizens. This is why I speak of a devaluation of the Going for Refuge. The Going for Refuge is really the central act of the Buddhist life. It is what makes you a Buddhist. But in popular, modern Buddhism it has largely become something peripheral, something formal, and something of purely cultural significance.

I think this is why it took me such a long time to see that it was on the basis of individual commitment that a new Buddhist movement must be founded. So far as I can remember, no one ever stressed to me the importance of Going for Refuge during the course of my entire stay in India. Some people were very particular indeed about the correct pronunciation of the Pali Refuge formula, but they paid no attention to what the words actually meant. I therefore had to discover the significance of the Going for Refuge for myself. When I had done this I saw that it was in fact the key to everything, saw that it was the basis of our new Buddhist movement. So in the FWBO tremendous emphasis is placed on the Going for Refuge. This is actually the simplest thing in Buddhism, but it is the most important.

The last reason that nobody had thought of starting an Order instead of yet another Buddhist organization had to do with an overvaluation of monasticism, especially of formal monasticism. If, nowadays, you were to ask a serious-minded Eastern Buddhist, especially from South-East Asia, what really makes one a Buddhist, more often than not he will say that the real Buddhist is the *monk*. He will say that if you really want to practise Buddhism you must become a monk; a layman cannot practise Buddhism—or he can do so only to a very limited extent. The best thing the layman can do is support the monks, supply them with food, clothing, shelter, and medicine. In this way the layman can earn some merit and hopefully, on the strength of that merit, be reborn in heaven after his death, or at least be reborn on earth in a rich family.

It would appear that, because the Going for Refuge has been *devalued*, monasticism has been *overvalued*, and over-emphasized. Being a Buddhist is no longer a matter of Going for Refuge, no longer a question of committing oneself to the Buddha, the Dharma, and the Sangha. Being a Buddhist means, in effect, becoming a monk. I most certainly do not want to undervalue monasticism or the monastic life— that would be going to the other extreme. I have been a monk myself for more than half my life, and I think that in many ways the life of a monk is the best possible kind of life. But to be a Buddhist it is not necessary to be a monk. What *is* necessary is that one should go for Refuge; what is necessary is the commitment to the Buddha, the Dharma, and the Sangha. That commitment is primary—lifestyle is secondary. For many people, of course, this commitment may find expression in the leading of a monastic life. This was particularly the case in the Buddha's own day, but even then it was not invariably the case. According to the Pali texts, some of the Buddha's followers attained a high level of spiritual development while continuing to live at home as laymen and laywomen. And of course, when I say that spiritual commitment can be expressed in the leading of the monastic life, I should perhaps add that by this I mean the leading of a *genuinely* monastic life. This unfortunately is not always the case. In many parts of Asia, commitment has been replaced by monasticism. And more often than not this is not genuine monasticism. More often than not genuine monasticism has been replaced by merely formal monasticism. The laity in many parts of the Buddhist world go through the motions of Going for Refuge, while in much the same way the monks go through the motions of being monks—which is to say they recite the monastic rules at intervals, without really asking themselves what those rules mean.

Perhaps we can now see why nobody had thought of starting an Order instead of yet another Buddhist organization. Seeing things from their own particular point of view they thought they already had an Order when they did not in fact have an Order at all. They had, in most places, just a number of people following the same life-style in an external, mechanical sort of way. However, as soon as you put the emphasis on Going for Refuge, monasticism is no longer over-valued. It takes its proper place as one possible life-style for the committed individual Buddhist.

We now have a clearer idea of the sense in which the WBO is an Order. It is a free association of committed individuals, of people who take Enlightenment as their ideal, who try to develop as individuals, who experience for themselves, in themselves, the successive stages of the spiritual path, who enjoy spiritual fellowship with one another, and who help, encourage, and inspire one another.

Some of these committed people in the Western Buddhist Order are old, some are young. Some are men, some are women. Some live in resident semi-monastic communities, others live at home with their families, and a few live on their own. Some live in the cities, some live in the country. Some are quite highly educated, some have no formal education at all. Some have a leaning towards the arts, some towards sciences. Some live in England, some live in Finland, some live in India, some in Europe, some in the USA, some in Australia, and some in New Zealand. But all are committed to the Buddha, all are committed to the Dharma, all are committed to the Sangha; all are united in Going for Refuge. All therefore belong to the same spiritual community, all are 'members' of the Western Buddhist Order.

It is these spiritually committed individuals, and these alone, who are responsible for running the different FWBO centres. It is not that members of the WBO *have* to run the centres— this is a matter of their own free choice. Some Order members have nothing whatever to do with the running of FWBO centres but get on with their own spiritual practice while keeping in regular touch with other Order members. But if, as an Order member, you want to start a centre of the FWBO, you just get together with half a dozen other Order members and agree among yourselves to set it up.

An important point to be made here is that, while there are many different FWBOs in different countries, they are all legally and financially independent. There is no single headquarters for the entire FWBO movement. Orders do not come from above. Actually, they do not come from anywhere. Local activities are run by local Order members. The unity of the movement is therefore spiritual rather than organizational. All Order members everywhere belong to the same Order, and the different centres are therefore run in the same spirit.

At this stage the question might arise as to how one becomes an Order member. In saying just a few words about this, I should also be able to explain the sense in which the FWBO is a movement of friends.

Let us suppose that an FWBO centre has been opened in your part of the world, and starts running meditation classes, Yoga classes, lectures, study groups, retreats, and so on—all the usual FWBO activities. And suppose it so happens that you get to know about it and go along in order to sample some of its activities. As soon as you come along you are reckoned as a

'Friend'—with a capital 'F'—of the Movement. You can come along as frequently or as infrequently as you please. You are not asked to join anything, you are not given any responsibility, you can just make whatever use you please of the centre's facilities: you are a Friend. The great majority of people in the FWBO are Friends. There might be quite a few tens of thousands of them who come along every now and then—in some cases for years—attending the odd class or lecture, or the occasional retreat, but without wanting to go any further than that.

Some, however, do want to go further. They start attending classes regularly, start meditating at home every day; they start bringing their working life into line with the principle of Right Livelihood. Maybe they will also help out at the centre from time to time, and make the effort to get into closer contact with Order members, until, in short, they start feeling that they 'belong' to the FWBO, and want to be more deeply involved. Such people can therefore become what we call 'mitras'. (The Sanskrit word *mitra* means simply 'friend', but the Sanskrit form is used in order to distinguish 'mitras' from 'Friends'.) One becomes a mitra in a simple ceremony in which the mitra-to-be offers a flower, a lighted candle, and a stick of incense to the Buddha image on the shrine. The ceremony usually takes place in the context of a *puja* (a sort of devotional ceremony)—usually on the occasion of a Buddhist festival—at the Centre, or perhaps away on retreat, in the presence of Order members, other mitras, and Friends.

Some people become mitras after just a few months as Friends; others wait for two or three or four years. Special study groups and special retreats are arranged for mitras, allowing them to have more contact with Order members and to intensify their practice. Again, some people find that being a mitra gives them all that they need, and may not wish to go any further than this. Others, however, will want to go further and will start thinking in terms of actual commitment. They may start thinking that they would like to commit their whole life to the Buddha, the Dharma, and the Sangha, that they would like to go for Refuge. There are those who reach this point after just a few months as a mitra, others reach it after a few years, but sooner or later some of them at least reach the point of asking for ordination into the Western Buddhist Order.

By now you should have a good general picture of the FWBO. As a total movement the FWBO consists of two 'parts'. Firstly there is the Order, the community of spiritually committed individuals. Secondly there are the Friends and the mitras. These Friends and mitras make up what we could call the 'positive group'. You will of course recall that I had some hard things to say about the group in my first talk. Those were,

I believe, fully justified. Nevertheless, we must not forget that there is such a thing as a positive group, which consists of people who are happy, healthy, and human. Above all, the positive group is open to the spiritual community. The FWBO is a movement of Friends in the sense that it includes a positive group of this sort, one that is open to the spiritual community.

*   *   *

In these three talks I have tried to communicate some idea of our new Buddhist movement. I have tried to explain in what sense it is Western, in what sense it is Buddhist, in what sense it is an Order, and in what sense it is a movement of Friends. It may seem as though I have told you quite a lot, but this is not really so. I have really given little more than a glimpse of the FWBO. If you want to know more then you will have to experience it personally, from within. I hope that you will do just that, and I hope that, having made contact with the FWBO, you will make a closer and closer contact with that current of spiritual energy which is our new Buddhist movement. And I hope that, sooner or later, you will allow that current to sweep you away.